T0196546

More Than
DIAMONDS
More Than
PEARLS

More Than DIAMONDS More Than PEARLS
You Are Worth It All

Written by

Keith L. Bell

Poems by William Wilson

Library of Congress Control Number: 2017900132
ISBN: Hardcover   978-1-5245-7445-1
                   Softcover   978-1-5245-7444-4
                   eBook   978-1-5245-7443-7

Rev. date: 01/05/2017

To order additional copies of this book, contact:
Xlibris
1-888-795-4274
www.Xlibris.com
Orders@Xlibris.com
752087

"If I Could"

If I could do anything in the world once, just one time, I would probably take a trip to Europe to visit Romania or to Italy to check out the old Roman Empire of Rome. Yeah, that sounds like royalty. But there must be something more superior than visiting Europe and Italy right? So...

If I could do anything in the world once, just one time, I would probably kick it with the president of the United States or instead of landing on the moon, I'll land on the sun. Nawl I couldn't do that because I'll burn to death before I got there so I'll shoot for the stars and become star struck, literally. Now that's extraordinary! But still, there must be something more extravagant than that, so…

If I could do anything in the world once, just one time, I would probably climb the highest mountain ever or scuba dive to the deepest part of the sea to see what's really down there or pass through the Bermuda Circle to see what's really on the other side. Now that's adventurous! But there still must be something more promising, so…

If I could do anything in the world once, just one time, I would probably end all poverty and feed every hungry stomach in the world or I would probably rewind the hands of time and go back a million years to when God first created the

Heavens and Earth and help Him bring the universe into existences. Yeah now that's promising and probably what I'll do!

But nothing I said in this poem was definite. Everything had "probably" in front of it. So If I could "DEFINITELY" do anything in this world once, just one time, I would bring my mother back. If it was only for a day, a hour, a minute, I would bring my mother back. If it was to only hug, hold and kiss her, I would bring my mother back. If it was to only say the things that were left unsaid or to do the things that were left undone, I would bring my mother back. Yeah that's exactly what I'll do. "If I Could" I'll bring my mother back.

-Keith L. Bell

Sisters, I'm here to be obtained, kept, and implemented into your lives. I'm here for y'all. I'm here for all, but all don't hear when I call. So I cry even louder, hoping to reach the ones that do not hear me.

Sisters, I come in different shapes, forms, and fashions, seeking to dwell in the minds of the people. I can be possessed by sight, by hearing, and by feelings. I can be shared among friends but seldom among children.

Whoever Loves Me Loves Life

Sisters, get knowledge, and in all of your getting, get understanding, and then you're on the right path to me. But until you use what you know, then I could never be.

Wisdom is my name, and I'm written all through the pages of this book. So take heed to the message as the writer pleas through his pen, trying to touch the hearts, fill the minds, and uplift the spirits of the women all over the world by first seeking revenge on every hurt, damage or strong hold. So that you're able to come to the realization that you are worth more.

Oh, beautiful strong women of all colors, shapes, and sizes, take hold of me, then hold on to me for dear life because the time is now to get what you deserve.

But you only get what you think you're worth . . .

INTRODUCTION

I'm writing this book More Than Diamonds More Than Pearls *You Are Worth It All* with high hopes of empowering and encouraging my sisters all over the world to become better individuals. I chose to use the word "sister" because that's exactly how I perceive each and every one of you—as a sister. No matter what color you may be or what language you may speak, *you* are my sister. You will see the word "sister" a lot throughout the text of this book, and the reason is so you'll know that I'm talking directly to you.

Since it's next to impossible for me to know and remember every female in the world, I'm also using the word "sister" as an indication for your name. So anytime you see the word "sister," replace it with your name. That way, you'll know that I'm talking directly to you.

I have two biological sisters, and I do not look at you any differently than I do them. And with that said, just like I want what's best for them, I also want what's best for you.

I'm going to be ingenious and straightforward with you throughout the text of this book so that you are able to fully grasp and conceive the concept and the message that I'm giving. I earnestly ask that you do not take the message of *You Are Worth It All* the wrong way because I've made it my personal goal to reach out and uplift my sisters by giving you insight and knowledge and to remind you of how much value you possess until you begin to discredit yourself. So when reading, please read with an open mind and heart.

I believe that in this day and time, a lot of women, both young and old, have great intentions but are strayed away from them and end up with an improper or wrong outlook in life after being misused, misguided, deceived by a man and or because of a lack of self-knowledge (knowing who you are and your self-worth). My intentions are to optimistically bring you up. Nothing I say in this book will be to discourage, dishearten, or depress you. Everything I say will simply be the truth and words of encouragement. Nothing should strike you as new in this book because nothing in this book has been created or discovered. Like I said, *You Are Worth It All* is all about enlightenment and upliftment. *You Are Worth It All* is about me giving you simple reminders that you are worthy of every great thing your heart desires.

Sisters, keep in mind that in order to achieve those great things your heart desires, you *must* live for a purpose. Rick Warren said it best when he stated that "There is nothing quite as potent as a focused life, one lived on purpose." So I'm challenging each and every one of you to stop selling yourself short and find out the purpose of your life and fulfill that purpose so that you are able to conquer those great things your heart desires and become a source of inspiration to others.

Now before I end the introduction, I want my sisters all over the world to remember you are just as worthy as every other successful person to live life abundantly.

A Voice of God's

My child, I'm always awake, waiting to hear your requests, to help alleviate your problems and clean up your mess. I'm your creator, your father, your provider, your shield. My child, listen when I speak because my guidance is real.

I'm the one that feeds the homeless and tells that man to give you that job. I am your endurance, your strength when times get hard. I will stand with you in fiery furnaces and protect you in a lion's den. I am a just God, a righteous God. My child, I am the forgiver of your sins.

All I ask for in return is your love, your obedience, your respect, and your praise.

To let my light shine in life, as you turn from the sins I forgave. My child, you either love me or you don't. There is no in between. My love is unconditional. I'll bring reality to your dreams.

You were put here for a purpose, something greater to be. I hope you find out what it is or later you will see. You may become tired in the process, but still, give me your all. It's okay if you fall. Keep your faith in me and know that I am here when you call.

My child, rise early and seek me and call upon my holy name. I promise to not only listen to your prayers but also answer them miraculously, easing your pain.

CHAPTER 1

Spiritual Foundation

"If you are not as close to God as you used to be, who moved?"

Now I'm not big on the preaching thing, sisters, because I've never really been the holy type. I've always been more of a spiritual person. So with that said, I believe that it's only right that we start this book and chapter off giving glory to our Creator, God, for creating us because without him doing such, we wouldn't be where we're at today.

I want each and every one of you who's reading this book to take a second *right now* to thank your God (even if all you say is "Thank you, God!") . . .

Amen. If you've noticed, I told you to thank "your God," and I said that because although I believe we all share the same God, we may call Him by different names. My God may be different from your God, and your God may be different from her God although I believe we all share the same God. Because God is just that—God.

But no matter your religion, belief, dogma, or tenet, rather you are a Christian, Muslim, Buddhist, or Jew, you pray to a God of some sort. Personally, I do not have one specific religion that I believe in. But that does not mean that I don't believe in a higher power because I do. I just believe (and this is just my belief) that as long as the religion we're following is teaching righteousness, there isn't a right or wrong religion that God wants us to follow. Remember, this is my standpoint. Yours may be a little different. I can go to any service held by any religion because when I go, I go to learn something from the speaker, something that I can incorporate into my daily life to help me grow as an individual. I just don't see how a religion could be a wrong religion if the religion is teaching its people righteousness, peace, justice, love and all the other good deeds of the world. I just don't see anything wrong with that. Do you? There are many religions teaching those deeds. For instance, on two different occasions, I met a guy and a woman, both studying Buddhism. We've all heard a story or two about Buddhism, but I promise you these people were more caring, giving, and humble than most. I'm saying this to say we should never judge a person's character by their religion.

I'm more into meditation because it keeps me intact with my higher self and keeps me sound. But when I pray, I pray to God, my God, who doesn't have a certain name. But like I said, sisters, these are my personal beliefs. Yours may be and are more than likely different from mine.

Having a spiritual foundation and some type of contact with your higher power or the God of your choice is critically essential, sisters. Without a spiritual foundation, your perception of life will be blurred, and so will your visions, dreams, and goals. But with God in your life, you'll have a clear sense of direction and guidance. Your visions, goals, and dreams will be transparent and seem within reach.

Build a foundation that's strong and solid with your God, sisters, so that you are comfortable talking with Him about the things your beautiful heart desires and the secrets that you hold on to so dearly. One way to build a strong foundation with your God is by sharing all your life experiences with him. Let him know about all your faults and failures, confess your sins (we all have them), and ask for forgiveness. Let him know about your achievements. Tell him when you are feeling discouraged and when you need his strength. Although God knows these things already, he still wants you to confess and talk to him about the experiences you face in life.

You know how you love to dump your problems on your man or best friend hoping to get some gratification? Well, let me tell you now God will listen to you with ears that will be opened a zillion times more than your best friend's or man's ears will ever be. And you know how sometimes your man and best friend may act as if they don't want to hear it? Well, God will *never* act that way. As a matter of fact, God is always ready and willing to hear it and heal it for you. God yearns to be more than your Creator and Maker, your Lord and Master, sisters. God also wants to be your friend. Do not think or feel like you aren't good enough to be friends with God because of a sin that you've committed either. You must remember that God is the forgiver of all sins. The Bible tells us that God was friends with sinners and that all have sinned and fell short to the glory of God. But God forgives. So the next time you feel like getting something off your chest, talk to God, your God, about it. You don't have to be praying while you're talking to God either, sisters. You can simply start a conversation with him like you would with your best friend or man. I guarantee you that once you are done talking to Him, it will feel as if you've talked to your man *and* your best friend because God is both of them and more, so much more.

God makes the impossible possible. God will give you the strength and will power you need when you think that you have none left. When things start to seem unbearable, God will make those things bearable. All you have to do is talk to him and truly believe and have faith in him. God will do things that you could never do for yourself. God is love, sisters. Love God with all of you. Give God all of you and He'll give you all of Him. I believe one of the main reasons all these tragic events where people are taking innocent lives—the school shooting in

Connecticut, the 9/11 attack, the Boston Marathon bombing, to name a few—are happening around the world is that those people who are responsible don't or didn't have any real spiritual grounding. They didn't know God. And if they did, they weren't applying the principles of God's teaching to their life. If they were, they wouldn't have as much as had the heart to kill the animals they eat, let alone a human being.

God created each and every one of you differently and for a purpose, sisters, and that alone should tell you that you are worth every great thing your heart desires. Never feel that you aren't worth something because of your circumstances or something that happened in the past because, sisters, you still are worth every great thing your heart desires. You must believe in yourself, sister. Even when no one else believes in you, keep the faith. Life is about growing and learning from the mistakes we make. Stagnation is a disease, don't catch it. God gives us the opportunity to do anything and everything our heart desires. He gives us the universe. Now that's *love.*

SIMPLE REMINDERS

1. Build a foundation that's strong and solid with your god so that you are comfortable talking with him about anything and everything.

2. Never judge a person's character by their religion.

3. With God in your life, you'll have a clear sense of direction and guidance. But without God, your perception will be blurry.

4. God is always ready and willing to hear your problems and alleviate them as well.

5. God makes the impossible possible, so trust and believe in him with all of you.

"Love and Believe"
"I Love and Believe In Myself"

No one can tell you different because it shows in your actions. Written all over your face, is the expression of satisfaction.

Satisfaction guaranteed is what we get from a woman who loves and believes. She stand her ground, her thoughts are sound. And the love she spreads around we need.

Her spirit is an inspiration to other women and her presence is the motivation to men. And even though all sin, she is still pure in the eyes of her children.

So shoot for the stars, but first know who you are. Believe in yourself with love, even when no one else does.

Because in order to get what is due, and for your dreams to come true, know that it all starts with you, so......

LOVE AND BELIEVE IN YOURSELF!

CHAPTER 2

Love and Believe in Yourself

If you don't like something change it, if
you can't change it, change the way you
think about it.

—Mary Engelbreit

To love and believe in ourselves is something
we humans do unconsciously. We don't have to
constantly remind ourselves to love ourselves; we
do it automatically. Some people just pay more
attention to the way they love themselves more
than others. That's why some people's lives are
better than others. Love, defined in *Webster's New
Dictionary,* is a passion or strong affection for

someone or something. So I believe it's safe to say that we all love ourselves to some extent.

Sisters, you must learn to love and believe in yourself even when no one else will or do because you can trust that there will be times when you feel alone and feel like nobody believes in you. This may cause you to become a little discouraged, but these are the times that you must stay strong and humbled, sisters. If not, the weight of the world may seem as if it's been placed on your shoulders, and it could cloud your vision and/or cause you to give up altogether. So never doubt yourself, sisters. Love yourself, and I mean really love yourself. That way, no matter what others may say about you, you'll always know that you are just as worthy as anybody else to live life bountifully.

Never let anyone intimidate you. You don't need permission from anyone to do something great. Maintaining belief and faith in yourself is essential. And always remember that your greatest weakness is a lack of self-confidence. Do not put others on a pedestal just because they're talented, have more experience, or have achieved great success before you. Doing so will leave you feeling less confident in your own abilities. So never stop loving and believing in yourself, sisters. Never compare your life with others or try to mimic others' success. Find your own path to success, sisters. Be great. Dream big but think bigger because you are just as worthy as anybody else to live life prosperously. But you have to be willing to go the extra mile to get ahead. *You* doing the necessary things with *your* time boils down to *you* living such a great life, sisters. Remember you can't recycle wasted time.

To love and believe in yourself requires more than just words, sisters. It requires action. So instead of saying how much you love yourself, show it by paying more attention to the smaller things we humans tend to overlook at times, such as what we put into our bodies, how we talk, how we think, and—this one we all tend to overlook a lot—how often we procrastinate.

Procrastination is one of the most common causes of failure, sisters. It stands within the shadow of every human being, waiting for the opportunity to spoil your chance at success. So stop procrastinating on doing the things that you need to do to get ahead. You know just as well as I know that once a task gets put off time and time again, that task becomes irrelevant. Most people go through life as failures because of waiting for the time to be just right to start chasing their dreams. Do not wait, sisters. The time will never be just right. Start where you stand and work with whatever you have to work with at the moment, and things will get better as you move along your journey.

Often it's the small things in life we humans overlook that hold us back, sisters. They say we are our own worst enemies, and I find that statement to be relatively true because there are many self-defeating behaviors that may cause one to self-destruct. The good thing about these behaviors, sisters, is we can overcome them once one have identified what the behaviors are. Not all of us share the same behaviors, and some may have more of these self-defeating behaviors than others, but one thing's for sure is we've all either had or have (because no one is perfect) some of these behaviors. But like I stated, these behaviors can be overcame, but one must first believe they can overcome the behaviors. That's key. Then knowing what causes the behavior gives us the ability to create or recreate a new way of reacting to the behavior. The behavior will only change once we learn to control the reaction to the behavior.

But I couldn't stress to you enough how vital truly loving and believing in yourself is, sisters. Listen, your family, your best friend, your teachers, and your man can have all the love in the world for you, they can believe in you like they believe in God, but if you don't have that same level of love and faith in and for yourself to do what's essential to elevate in life, you'll constantly feel that you are not good enough to prevail and live life flourishingly. And with that feeling, you will become content with the life you are living instead of reaching higher and striving for more. So love yourself, sisters, and never lose faith. Remember, in order to rise, we must think high.

Education is very important when it comes to believing in yourself, sisters. Why? Because the more you know about your goal or what it is that you want out of life, the more confidence you'll have in your abilities to accomplish them. Confidence is also key. There's nothing or no one standing in the way, stopping you or holding you back, but *you*! Think about this for a second: If a man who has prosthetic legs can race in the Olympics with enough faith in himself, believing that he could win, then what's stopping you from chasing your dreams? Life's not about stagnation. Life's about evolving. It's about giving back and helping others. But without the proper love for yourself, those things will seem very farfetched, sisters. And the attitude you will possess will be unfavorable and tainted and will leave you stuck wondering why no one wants to be around you. Love and positivity go hand in hand and usually attracts the same thing just as hate and negativity do.

If you don't love and believe in yourself, who will, sisters? Don't think for a second that your man will because he won't, and neither will your so-called friends. Love is an emotion that must be reciprocated. In short, you have to give love to receive love, and in order to give it, you must truly have it within yourself. How could you give something you don't have? You can't. It's impossible. So love yourself first so that you will be able to give love to the world that's waiting with open arms to love you back. A woman that's loving to the world is like a brand new set of tires and a tune-up to a car; she makes things run smoothly. Remember that!

SIMPLE REMINDERS

1. Remember that nothing or no one will be able to deter you from living life potentially when you "really" love yourself.
2. Show how much you love yourself instead of saying it.
3. You'll know that you are just as worthy as anybody else to live life abundantly when you "truly" believe in yourself. So believe, sisters!
4. The time will never be just right for you to start chasing your dreams. START NOW!
5. There's nothing or no one standing in your way or stopping you from reaching your full potential but *you*.

APPERANCES

Woman: Look at me, I look good!

Man: I'm looking at you but not the way you think I should.

Woman: Don't I look sexy in my gear?

Man: Yes, but where are you going? Because you are sexy still without your body parts showing. Sexy is your attitude, swagger, and confidence, loving yourself and being lovable without the approval of an audience.

Woman: You must not know my motto: "If you got it, might as well flaunt it."

Man:	I know that if you have it, you are blessed. But flaunting it can bring things unwanted. What are you seeking, sista?
Woman:	I just want some attention.
Man:	Attention? Well, be careful because the wrong kind will bring things I just mentioned.
Woman:	So what, you don't like what I got on?
Man:	Oh, I like it but not like that. I wouldn't dare let my woman put that on because that alone would lose her respect. Now, sista, I respect you, but you should respect yourself first. When you dress like that, showing too much, you are only showing signs of thirst.

Just remember that your appearance is what you appear to be. So if you are showing all you got, then that must be all you have. And these are the thoughts from all I see.

CHAPTER 3

Appearances

"The real ornament of a woman is her character and her purity."

—Mohandas Gandhi

Appearances, appearances, appearances. Now, sisters, I'm sure each and every one of you know exactly what appearances are. But if you don't, your appearance is everything showing on the outside of your body, i.e., the way you dress, the way you look.

Now I know every one of you love to look good because looking good is human nature. Besides, when you're looking good, you're feeling good, and when you're feeling good, everything just feels right, right? Right. But remember there's a certain way that you and your appearance gets perceived when you're looking good, sisters. I'm sure most of you know that already, but some of you still dress like you don't. Or is it that you just don't care?

Men love women with class, who know how to dress sexy appropriately, sisters. Too much showing of the skin and you are automatically stereotyped as someone with low class and easy to get with. But more importantly, you'll be seen as somebody not to take seriously. Sisters, you can be the most innocent person to ever walk the face of this earth, with the greatest intentions ever, with a heart of gold, but if your appearance isn't speaking those same volumes of you, then no one may ever even think to know those things about you. We're living in a world where people judge books by their covers. Your physical being is the book, and your appearance is the cover. So people are judging you by what they see, not by what they know.

See, there's a certain type of sexy that's perceived as ladylike, sisters. You don't have to dress in the least clothing as possible to dress sexy. As a matter of fact, your entire body can be covered and you can still be sexy because sexy isn't just the skin that the eyes see, just like beauty isn't just what the mind sees.

Now there's nothing wrong with showing a little skin because men also love women who are comfortable with their body, sisters. But too much showing of the skin is never a good sign in a man's eyes. I say too much showing of the skin is a turn-on and a turn-off all at the same time for us men. And I'll explain. I say it's a turn-on because a man will see all that skin and immediately begin to imagine what it's like to have you in bed. Nothing more, nothing less. I mean, think about it, there's not a *man* on earth who could see a half-dressed woman and his first thoughts be to marry her, which leads me right into my next conclusion. I say it's a turn-off because the part of the man's brain that does the thinking, considering, and judging sees too much skin, and it's like a lightbulb goes off telling the man that *all* you may be worthy of is sex when, actually, you are worthy of more than what your appearance say about you. Long story short, you're in a lose-lose situation with a man when you have to much skin showing, sisters. Whatever manner you choose to dress in will be the same manner you'll be perceived as. Remember that. You must dress more adequately and stop leaving little to the imagination of men because the more you show, the less men think of you. And that's pure honesty.

Okay, now that we know that appearance plays a major role in one's confidence and self-esteem level, and that the way we dress affects the way we feel, I want to mention one of the most common reasons women dress covering their body so disgracefully to begin with—for attention. Women love attention. I repeat, women love attention! Trust me, I know.

I grew up in a household with two sisters and a mother, so I know just how much attention women love. Now there's nothing wrong with wanting some attention, sisters, because I believe every woman deserves it. But when you aren't getting the attention you're seeking or the gratification you deserve, sisters, you must stop showing your body off to get it. That's one of the biggest mistakes you can make as a woman. Doing such, you are only discrediting and demoralizing yourself, which often opens the door for men to discredit and demoralize you.

So, sisters, please stop showing your body off to get the attention you are seeking and focus that energy on doing something productive to bring the attention that you are seeking about. You must give yourself the utmost respect, sisters. If you don't, nobody will. Or think about it like this: The amount of respect that you give yourself will be the same amount that you get back. Give the world your all. Don't take any shortcuts with yourself. There are no shortcuts to success, sisters. It's a way of life. I once heard someone say "Success is a mind-set, not a point in time." And that makes all the sense in the world if you actually think about it.

Sisters, also keep in mind that your younger sisters are looking up to you, watching the way you carry yourself. So dressing inappropriately will give them the impression that it's okay to dress in that same manner. So be the grown woman that you want them to look up to.

It's a known fact that a lot of younger females are dressing so inappropriately, to begin with, because they want to give themselves an older look, which is nothing but a lack of guidance and immature thinking. There are fourteen-year-olds trying to look eighteen and eighteen-year-olds trying to look twenty-five. But there aren't any twenty-five-year-old women trying to look like thirty-year-old women. And I wonder why. Well, I know why, and it's because once you reach a certain age, you no longer want to look older anymore. You then begin wanting your younger look back. Think about it, aren't older women getting surgery done so they can look young again? That alone should tell you something. So stay young and look young while you can, sisters. Aging is inevitable; it's something that's going to happen regardless of what you do. All you have to do is be patient and continue to live your life, and just as sure as the sky is blue, you will turn that certain age you're so anxious to be. I promise you will.

Until then, sisters (my younger sisters), I humbly say to you that time moves fast and that you'll only be fourteen once. So do the things that of which a fourteen-year-old child does while you can because in the blink of an eye, you'll be wishing that you could do it all over again. But with age, just like life, there aren't any do overs. So, sisters, please take your life seriously and stop aging yourself before you actually age because life is short and aging yourself only shortens it.

However, before I end this chapter, I want to remind my sisters all over the world that your appearance speaks things beyond words about you. Remember, people judge books by their covers. You are the book, and your appearance is the cover to the book. So people are judging you by what they see, not by what they know about you.

SIMPLE REMINDERS

1. People are judging you by what they see, not by what they know.
2. Too much showing of the skin is never a good sign in a man's eyes. With too much skin showing, you are in a lose-lose situation with a man.
3. Your younger sisters are watching you, so be the grown woman you want them to look up to.

4. The manner you choose to dress in is the same manner you will be perceived as. So please start dressing more adequately, sisters.

5. Sexy is not just the skin that the eyes see.

"ATTITUDE"

My attitude can take me whenever I want to go, and it can also prevent me from going. It's one of the seeds that breed life and death. And I choose to live.

Being alive is so much better than death or just waiting to die. My thoughts, my words, and my spirit is what shapes my life. And each individual element alone can kill my being.

So I try to stay mindful of them all as they change with speed, because my subconscious mind and my feelings have no time frame.

But I have one. I'm in control of my life and my destiny, I am a conqueror. Overcoming all challenges with a finesse that expresses success.

I am facing my realities as I head towards my dreams. Leaving behind fragments of my attitude planted in the minds of the people I come in contact with.

I'm making the best of all moments in life because I've got places to go, people to meet and things to do, so this is my attitude.

It's going to get me where I'm destined to go, because the choice is mine!

Can you guess which attitude I possess?

CHAPTER 4

A Positive Attitude versus a Negative Attitude

If you don't like something change it, if you can't change it, change the way you think about it.

—Mary Engelbreit

Okay, now that I've mentioned a few things about the importance of having a spiritual foundation, loving and believing in yourself and appearances, I want to talk about the importance of knowing the different effects a positive attitude and a negative attitude have on those things. The first part of the chapter will be based on positive

attitudes and its benefits, and the next segment will
be on negative attitudes.

Attitude is defined as the mental position that
represents an individual's degree of like or dislike
for something, which is generally a positive or
negative view of a person, place, or thing.

A Positive Attitude:

First and foremost, sisters, your attitude reveals
the real you. And next to knowing God, nothing is
more important than having to a positive attitude.
Your attitude is the driving force of your life, sisters.
It has the ability to make or break you, heal or hurt
you. Your attitude has the ability to befriend you
with others or make you enemies with others. It
has the power of making you happy or miserable.
More importantly, your attitude plays a major part
on determining if you will become a success or a
failure, sisters. That may sound harsh, but it's the
truth.

A positive attitude and positive thinking heighten one's chances at prosperity. A positive attitude also increases productivity, solves problems that you may be facing, breeds loyalty and integrity, increases profits, and reduces stress levels. Think about it: it's hard to stay productive when you're stressed out.

That's only a few of the benefits of having a positive attitude. A positive attitude has the power to improve and change your life dramatically, sisters. However, your way of thinking, either positive or negative, is only a habit, and habits can be broken. Your thoughts are always under your control, sisters. Remember that. Positive people possess a certain attitude and personality traits that are easily recognized. These people are caring, confident, patient, and humble. So just because negativity is obsolete from your life, sisters, it doesn't necessarily make you a positive person. You must carry the traits of a positive person as well. And no matter how positive of a person you are, sisters, there will always be negativity and negative people trying to bring you down. Don't let it happen. Remain strong.

Overall, people with positive attitudes are optimistic and they believe they are accountable for good things and that good things will generally come their way. If bad things come instead, they brush it off as a sole incident and continue to believe that things will be better in the future. Optimistic people have the tendency to take the most hopeful views of matters, staying positive. Besides, people with positive attitudes simply live longer, happier, healthier, and more successful lives. Now who in their right mind doesn't want that? Another thing to remember about a positive attitude is that it is seen as a motivator. And with it, you much easily inspire others to perform at their best, which improves productivity with the human race. Numerous of studies have been conducted on optimism, and almost all came to the same conclusion: optimism is healthy! I do my best to stay positive in negative situations all because I know what it is that I truly want out of life.

I'm still growing and will continue to for as long as I live, and I encourage each and every one of you to do the same. Staying true to yourself, sisters, is something that you have to do when you're looking to grow. Finding and incorporating your real purpose in life will help you overcome just about any difficulty you face. When you are faced with hardship, if you know why your life is important, sisters, you will begin approaching difficult situations more boldly, only because you know that you are living for a purpose and nothing or no one shall ever stop you from fulfilling your purpose. Your confidence level rises once you've found out your purpose. The only person you should be worried about having confidence in your dreams is you. The rest will become believers once your dreams become realities. So don't ever feel that you need others to see your vision the way you see it because most won't, not even your family. And that's okay. That's why it's called *your* dream. So if you have a passion for something, go after it with pure faith and determination, no matter what others think.

A Negative Attitude:

For a start, sisters, negative thinking makes you feel bad in the present. Not only that, but also a negative attitude hinders your life's progress and severely limits your life's satisfaction and happiness. People with negative attitudes are usually bitter, resentful, and angry. They normally live a purposeless life, have bad health and high stress levels. People with negative attitudes have a hard time keeping friendships and relationships. Not only that, but also they unknowingly pass off their negative behavior to others.

Sisters, no more effort is required to aim high in life, to demand abundance and prosperity, than is required to accept misery and poverty (that's a quote from Napoleon Hill that I'll never forget), just like no more effort is required to think positive and possess a positive attitude than to think negative and possess a negative attitude. In other words, the same amount of energy is required to think negative or positive. It's just the choice you'll have to make. And sometimes the choices we make are done unconsciously, doing things without putting much thought into our actions, living purposelessly. People who nurture a consistently negative attitude, one who's always expecting the worst of situations and others, are called pessimistic people. Pessimistic people and adversity go hand in hand. Where there's one, there's always the other.

Sisters, the remarkable thing about attitude is we have a choice every second of the day as to what kind of attitude we possess. We cannot change our past, and this I know. But we can change our present to make a better future. We can change our attitude and outlook on life to make life better, not only for ourselves but for the people around us as well.

A negative attitude and negative thinking leads you down the wrong road, sisters, and is one of the fastest ways to self-destruct.

In closing this chapter, sisters, I want to give a few good words of advice to help create a more positive attitude. And the first piece of advice is to let go of the assumption that the world is against you because an assumption is all that thought is. It's not true. Although things may not be working out in your favor or going as planned, that does not mean that the world is against you, sisters. The entire world does not even know who you are to be against you. That's just negative thinking. One great thing about this life we live is the ones you feel are against you, *you* always have the ability to disassociate yourself from them and never be bothered with them again.

So, sisters, please stop thinking that the world is against you because it's not against you. I promise you, it's not. The world is actually for you. Some *people* in the world may be against you but not the world. God gives the toughest battles to his toughest soldiers. Nothing in life that's worth keeping comes easy. So if you are continuing to face some type of dilemma in accomplishing your goals, keep going! Don't give up! You must have an incredible state of endurance. I promise you it's going to feel that much better once you look back at the things you overcame. And once you convert your negative thinking into positive thinking, the easier it'll be to change your perspective on situations. You must also understand that the past does not equal the future, sisters. You must learn to use your past as a learning experience, a way to grow. Just because you were faced with misfortune in the past, doesn't mean you'll be faced with it in the future. Believe in yourself, sisters, with everything that you are made of! See yourself as a cause, sisters, never an effect. Stop thinking about what is happening to you and start thinking about what you can make happen. Use your negative experiences to build character and make better decisions, sisters. Self-elevation is key. I'm not suggesting that you become a Pollyanna, pretending nothing bad can or will ever happen, because doing so will lead to poor decision making and will also invite people to take advantage of you. Instead, I'm insisting you be a rational optimist, one who takes the good with the bad while knowing the good will always outweigh the bad and that the bad was only a bump in the road or another obstacle standing in the way, which actually gives us the chance to restrategize on the plans we've worked on to accomplish our goals.

Sisters, when you feel negativity clouding your judgment, or you start to feel down about the future or your current situation, remind yourself that every minute counts and any time spent brooding over negativity guarantees nothing but less time to enjoy whatever it is that life has to offer you.

> "Change your negative attitude
> into positive ones and you
> can change your world."

SIMPLE REMINDERS

1. A positive attitude and positive thinking heighten one's chances of prosperity.
2. Stop thinking about what's happening to you and start thinking about what you can make happen.
3. Your attitude reveals the real you.
4. No more effort is required to possess a positive attitude than is required to possess a negative attitude.
5. Your attitude is the driving force to your life.

"KEEPING SIGHT"

What I can see is closer to achieve.
Even if the whole world don't believe.

Everyone can have one. You, me, and
even the blind.
Because it's not what you can see through
your eyes but what you can conceive in
your mind.

This is my vision, my dreams, my goals.
And I've set out on a mission until things
unfold.

Fighting against Murphy's Law, as I hear
success voice.
And I choose to win, thank God I have
a choice.

Inspired by the liberty of my country,
the land of the free.
Where you can bring life to your
thoughts and make them entities.

So I create with my mind and zoom in
on my target.
I won't settle for nothing less than
success and there's no room to bargain.

I will not stand in my own way, because
it's all on me.
I see it, the end, the light, my life, my
destiny.

Chapter 5

Keeping Sight

Life is not the way it's supposed to be,
it's the way it is. The way you deal with
it is what makes the difference.

—Virgina Satir

In this chapter, sisters, I'm going to talk about the importance of having a vision and keeping sight of it. But first, let's make sure you know and understand just what a vision is. A vision is the mental image of what you see and want to do with your life, sisters. Once you've discovered your vision, you should develop a passion or strong desire for your vision sisters. And depending on how deep of a passion or desire you develop to bring your vision into reality will determine if your vision will be weak or strong. The less passion you have for your vision, the weaker your vision will be, and the more far away it will seem. But the more passion you have for your vision, the stronger your vision will be, and the clearer it will seem. If you are creating a vision that has no real incentive or significance, sisters, chances are your vision will not last because the only visions that last are visions that are rooted in value.

"Dreams and Goals"

Now, sisters, I know and pray that every one of you have a dream or dreams to become something(s) in life; it's human nature. We all want to be a "somebody." Rather, your dreams are to become the next big movie star, music star, or even a lawyer or doctor. Your dreams can and are actually meant to come true. But dreams don't come true from merely wishing and hoping, sisters. You must put the work in! If all you're doing is wishing and hoping that your dreams come true, sisters, take my advice and stop now! Because if you don't, you'll be wishing and hoping for a lifetime. And if you are thinking that you aren't lucky enough to become successful, *great thinking* because being lucky has nothing to do with your achievements. It's all about your drive. Not all successful people are gifted with talents, most just work hard, study a certain field then succeed on purpose. Call anybody that's successful lucky, and they will more than likely tell you that luck has nothing to do with the way their life turned out. Keeping sight and hard work mixed with persistence, dedication, and self-discipline blended with knowledge, passion, and patience wrapped in open-mindedness, fearlessness, and integrity is a fraction of what it takes to become successful. Luck has nothing to do with it. It's more like chance. Personally, I don't believe in luck, only blessings.

But keep faith in yourself, sisters, and chase after your dreams with pure persistence and determination. NEVER GIVE UP! Plot, plan, and strategize until you "arrive." Hard work pays off and will be well worth it in the end. Trust me.

Visions

Visions are easily blurred sisters, so please do not let nothing or nobody distract you or cause you to lose sight of your vision, not your family, not your friends, not even your man, if you have one. Keep a vivid picture of your vision in your mind, sisters. It's extremely important to keep a crystal-clear picture of your vision in your mind so that your vision will not deteriorate.

Sisters, if you ever feel like life has taken its toll on you, I encourage you to keep on keeping on and not get discouraged on your dreams and goals to the point of wanting to give up. Because life have the tendency to put people that has big dreams through the toughest tests. And life may be testing you at the moment to see just how much you can bare before it gives you that which your heart desires (God's work). Keep in mind that your dream is right around the corner from the point of where you are ready to give up from. So keep *pushing forward*, sisters, because God will never put too much on you that you can't handle.

See, life was designed for everyone to enjoy. It's not just for certain people. But the thing is, everyone is wanting to enjoy life while certain people are doing what's essential to enjoy it. And for this very same reason, everyone's not enjoying life. You have to really want to enjoy life to enjoy it. Remember that. Again, nothing in life worth having and keeping will come easy, sisters. So like president Barack Obama said in his 2013 inauguration speech, "We must learn more, work harder, and reach higher"; not a lot of words but some powerful ones.

I must admit that life isn't easy, sisters, and that nothing comes free. But in that same breath I must also admit that with our freedom to do whatever it is we choose to do with our life, life is as only as hard as we make it. Like I stated in chapter 4, your attitude and thought process play a major role on how your life turns out. Positive thinking and a positive attitude will take you a lot further in life than negative thoughts and a negative attitude will. For instance, a pessimistic person will experience adversity faster than an optimistic person would, only because the things you think about, you bring about, which is a known fact. If you're familiar with the Bible, it tells you in Proverbs 4:23 to "Keep your heart filled with all diligence, for out of it springs the issues of life."

Besides, walking around with a negative attitude is so unladylike sisters. No one wants to be around someone whose outlook in life is careless and thoughtless.

Knowing your self-worth, who you are, and what it is you want out of life will help you ultimately prevail over any careless or thoughtless thoughts you may have, sisters. Know your worth, sister! Do you know *your* self-worth? Are you placing a dollar amount on your self-worth? I sure hope not, sisters, because your self-worth is priceless. You and only you can determine your self-worth. Remember that. Never let another individual help you determine your self-worth!

In closing this chapter, I want you to always remember that you will know that you have discovered your purpose when the vision of your dream is constantly on your mind and heart. Never lose sight of this purpose! Utilize it so that you are able to help not only yourself but others as well. Visions that are rooted in value are the only visions that will last, sisters. Hold on to those words . . .

SIMPLE REMINDERS

1. Visions are easily blurred so don't let nothing or no one distract you.

2. It's all about your drive. Being lucky has nothing to do with your achievements.

3. Keep the faith in yourself and chase after your dreams with pure persistence and determination.

4. Take action because dreams don't come about from wishing and hoping.

5. Visions that are rooted in value are the only visions that will last.

"Just Talk"

Let me talk to you for a sec, and stimulate your intellect.

Giving you food for the thought as I share and just talk.

Did you know that 50% of marriages fail within the first year?

Let me say it one more time, 50%, just to make things clear.

Now, I'm wondering why most don't make it,

Because that's a big percentage for something so sacred.

What about the 80% of women who get abused and just take it?

Or the 63% of the women who are aids patients?

Every year 1.2 million students drop out of school?

And over 60% of the fathers are doing bids, that's probably why the kids think it's cool. So open your eyes, and take your time, and you'll probably find this true. That 67% of the babies are being molested by the people you "thought" you knew.

Is these percentages true or false, and do you believe it or doubt it?

If they are true and you knew, would you do something about it?

And no I'm not judging or displaying people's faults.

This is true and I shout it, this is not just talk!

CHAPTER 6

Just Talk

When you know you are of worth—not asking for it but knowing it—You walk into a room with a particular power. When you know you are of worth, you don't have to raise your voice, you don't have to become rude, you don't have to become vulgar, you just are. You are like the sky is, as the air is, the same way water is wet. You don't have to protest.

—Maya Angelou

In this final chapter, sisters, I just want to talk with you about a few things, things that I may have mentioned something about in one of the previous chapters. If I have, that's okay. It only means one thing, and it's vital that you take heed.

The first thing I'd love to say to my sisters all over the world is always stand up for what you believe in, even if standing alone is your only option. And *never* give up on your dreams. Continue to strive for what's right, and eventually, your dreams will unfold, slowly but surely. Remember, things will not go as planned one hundred percent of the time, so be prepared to face some adversity and some rejections along the way, sisters. It's going to happen. It still happens to me to this day. I look at adversity as a challenge. It makes me want to restrategize my plans and attack that situation until I've conquered it. Don't let road blocks or tree stomps restrain you from keeping on, sisters. Every failure brings with it the opportunity to succeed. Never be afraid of failure, sisters. Be afraid of never trying because you'll never know what your capabilities are until you try. So always try and don't give up if you fail. Try again and again until you succeed. Every action has a reaction, whether it's good or bad, and every reaction gives you the opportunity to learn from it as long as you are open-minded and tolerant toward the situation. And, sisters, please *think* before you *act*. Never act out of anger or other negative emotions because the decision making is always poor in those times and your actions will often leave you feeling regretful afterward. And when dealing with men sisters, intricate yourself a little if you have to. Never give a man the guidebook to your heart and what makes you happy. In other words, don't give him all of you at once. Let him find out some of the things about you on his own, and he will more than likely cherish those things more. And, sisters, make sure your endeavors at keeping a positive mind state, are always thoughtful even when you are surrounded by negativity. That task may seem as if it's hard to tackle at times, but remember, it's not impossible. Keep your spirits rich, sisters. And never do things that you would be ashamed to talk about afterward.

Sisters, integrity should be more than just a word that's in your vocabulary. It should be a word that you pride yourself on. Honesty, trustworthiness, fairness, completeness, sincerity, honor, and rectitude are all synonyms of the word integrity. Integrity is a function of your character, and your character is something that's not easily changed. Your character is a reflection of who you truly are. So make sure the essence of your character is based on integrity, sisters. There's a saying that goes something like "Be more concerned with your character than your reputation because your character is what/who you *really* are and your reputation is merely what others *think* you are. Some people tend to get their character and their reputation mixed up, thinking that they are the same, but there is a very distinct difference between the two, as one is who you are and the other is who others think you are. Other people's opinions should never dictate the way you feel about yourself unless they are great ones.

And, sisters, make sure your character is as modest, pure, and free from deception as possible because it's not only the man who's deceiving.

I also want to speak about the mind-set of "needing" a man that some of you possess, sisters. You should never feel that you need a man. It should be more of an "I'm ready" for a man mind state that you possess, sisters. I say that because you begin losing your independence once you begin to rely on a man or feel like you need a man. Once you begin to feel that you are ready for a man in your life, you know that you've got it together and is ready to take it to the next level or a step further in life without becoming dependent.

And, sisters, please stop trying to force relationships to work. If it's meant for the two of you to be, God will see that the two of you be together. Forcing the relationship or trying to make the relationship work will often result in you (not him) making sacrifices that you know aren't right. But you'll make them anyway only because you are forcing things to work out. Instead of letting things flow, you force them to flow just to make him happy, which is not, and I repeat, is not a healthy thing to do because it will be you who's giving your all while he's not even giving it his half.

If you are making these unhealthy sacrifices just to make your man happy, sisters, *stop*! If he's really worth it, you wouldn't be making these sacrifices alone. He would be making these sacrifices with you. Part 2 to this book is called "Is He Worth It?" and it goes into detail about finding out if a man is worth you being with. So make sure you check it out.

Another thing I want to encourage my sisters all over the world to do is stop complaining about the things you dislike about your life and start working on changing those aspects, instead of constantly complaining about them. You and only you have the power to change those things. If there's something you want out of life, you have to *get up and go get it,* sisters! Nothing will be handed to you. One of the surest ways to get it (whatever it is you want out of life) is first by knowing exactly what it is you want then keep sight of it and set goals that you must make plans for and follow through with absolute determination. And when following through with your plans, remember that short-term sacrifices must be made in order to capitalize on long-term opportunities that lie ahead. They say people that don't set goals never reach their full potential and effortlessly wander through life without making any real progress. I'm sure none of you want to be that person. So don't only set yourself some goals but follow through on the plans to accomplish those goals persistently.

With all this said, know your self-worth, sisters. If you don't know your self-worth find out what it is and cherish it. Consistently work on your personal development as a woman as well so that you are forever growing. Learn to be patient, and maintain faith in your own potential.

Last thing before ending this book, sisters, I want to leave you with two chapters as a bonus from "Is He Worth It?" and something that you should know already, which is you are going to come across men in your life who will say all the right words at all the right times, but in the end, it's always his actions you should judge him by. It is actions, not words, that matter most. So, sisters, if your man's words aren't lining up with his actions, ask yourself, "Is he worth it?" After reading this book, you know that you are worth "More Than Diamonds, More Than Pearls. You Are Worth It All."

SIMPLE REMINDERS

1. Pride yourself on integrity.

2. Never give up! Keep on keeping on, no matter how hard it gets.

3. Set goals for your plans and follow through on them with absolute determination.

4. Instead of complaining about the aspects you dislike about your life, work on changing them.

5. Know your self-worth. Never force relationships to work. Check out "Is He Worth It?"

BONUS CHAPTER

CHAPTER 1

Sex Isn't Everything

Now the body is not for fornication but
for God, and God for the body.

—Corinthians 6:13

Sisters, I'm pretty sure that each and every one of you know already that sex isn't everything and that it is actually a sin to fornicate (to fornicate simply means to have sexual intercourse without being married). Now I know that the majority of my sisters that read this book will be guilty of fornication, and that's okay. It doesn't make you a bad person. No one is perfect. We all make mistakes. Asking God for forgiveness is key. But, sisters, there must come a time when you leave the childish acts behind and stop giving yourself up so readily.

If you are with a man and you know deep down inside that he's not the one you see yourself with fifty years from now, why are you with him? You are wasting your precious time, time that you will never get back. It doesn't matter how beneficial he may be or seem to you at the moment. The question is, is he worth you wasting your time with just to find out that he was only there for sex? Probably not. Just because you give yourself to a man doesn't mean that he will care for you, sister. And chances are, the feelings he says he has for you aren't genuine, so after he gets what he wants from you, his interest may decrease, especially if it came easy.

See, men lose all respect for women who are easy to get and will continue to have sex with her only because she allows him to, not because he likes her or sees a future with her. So, sisters, I deeply suggest that you know what you are getting yourself into when dealing with men (the wrong men) because it will be you who's giving your all when he's only looking at you as a sex object.

Now I know that some of you are probably thinking, "It's his lost, not mine. He got played for his benefits and didn't get nothing in return," which may be true to a certain extent because, with all honesty, what he gave was material and far less valuable than what you gave, which is yourself and your body. You gave him *you*. So let's be truthful here—who really got played? All I'm saying here, sisters, is you have to change the way you are thinking, if this is the way you think, because the cycle will continue if you don't. And the longer the cycle continues, the worse your name will become. A good name means more to a man than good looks do any day. So please stop the cycle before it's too late, sisters, because no man even considers being with a woman who has a bad name or reputation. For instance, when a female has a title that comes with her name, such as "Freaky Jane" or "Nasty Natalie," it's hard for a man to take her seriously, relationship-wise, because of the title she have been labeled with. So please respect yourself enough not to mess around with every man you come in contact with, sisters, because it's easy to get labeled but hard, if not impossible, to get the label off. So just because a man took you out on a few dates or bought you nice things, doesn't mean you have to have sex with him in return. And if he insists that you do, you should stay away from him fast because, right off, you know what his intentions are.

Sisters, you must not fall for a man's looks either. Just because a man is dressed nicely and drives a nice car, it doesn't mean that man has his life together. Get to know who you are dealing with. You can tell what type of man you are dealing with a lot of the time from the way he walks, talks, and carries himself. It's common sense, sisters. It's simply good guys and bad guys in this world.

There's no in between. So if a guy approaches you like, "What's up, baby gurl? Let me holla at you for a second," you can categorize this type with the bad guys. His choice of words says it all. But if a guy approached you respectfully, saying something like "Excuse me, Miss, my name is William, and I couldn't help but notice how beautiful you are. Can I have a minute of your time, please?" you should still be cautious because men are masterly smooth, but you can more than likely categorize him with the good guys. But, sisters, if you aren't interested simply say so kindly instead of leading him on because you don't want to be mean and hurt his feelings. That's how unwanted friendships lead to relationships, which often lead to breakups, broken hearts, and children being raised in single-parent homes instead of two.

I have a question, sisters. I can't seem to understand why is it that when a good guy (which for some reason gets called a lame or some name like that) approaches you, he gets turned down? But when the bad guy approaches you, he gets some play when you already know that he's not going to do right? I never understood that. It just doesn't add up and doesn't make sense to me. You will come in contact with a good man and run all on top of him then come in contact with a guy who shatters your already broken heart and can't seem to get enough of him, which leaves you saying things like "There aren't any good men out here" or "All men are the same." I wonder why.

From me to you, sisters, the good guy who you turned down is 99.9 percent more likely to be the one for you versus the bad guy who you just can't seem to stay away from. You have to learn to try something new if you want new results. I can almost guarantee you that the good guy will protect and provide for you just as much as the bad guy will, if not more. Then having your heart broken will be the last thing on your mind. Besides, the only place the bad guy can take you that the good guy can't is the hood, and who haven't seen that already? So keep in mind that while the bad guy is showing you the hood, Mr. Good Guy has potential of showing you the world. Think about it.

But back to the subject at hand, sisters. It's extremely important that you remember that sex isn't everything and that you aren't only sinning but selling yourself short giving yourself away. You degrade yourself even more when you give yourself away to a man who you are not even in a relationship with, sisters. You are only setting yourself up to be used. And, sisters, if you have multiple sex partners, ask yourself why and come up with an answer other than "Because I want to" or "Because I'm grown." You must ask yourself, is the man you're having sex with the guy you see yourself marrying? Better yet, find out if his intentions are to settle down and marry *You*. If not, you should be asking yourself the biggest question of all sisters, which is "Is He Worth It?"

"Men will tell you everything
you want to hear to have
sex with you . . . Don't fall
for the okiedokie."

CHAPTER 2

"Main Squeeze/Main Thing or Only Thing"

Life is 10 percent of what happens to us
and 90 percent of how we react to it . . .
—Dennis P. Kimbro

Sisters, the title of which your man gives you is very important. It means a lot and says a lot as well. Trust me, I know. I used to do the name-calling thing. It may not seem like the name your man calls you means much, but trust me, it does. For instance, if your man calls you his "main squeeze" or his "main thing," chances are you aren't his "only thing." Think about it: The word "main" means "mostly," and a synonym for the word "main" is "first," so if you're his "main squeeze" or "main thing," then you are mostly his first girl. And if you are mostly, then you are not his all, and just because you are first, it doesn't mean there aren't any seconds.

You will probably never hear your man call you anything other than your government name, baby, or the cute little nickname he gave you when the two of you first met because the other titles he will only refer to you as when he's out with his friends. But if you ever happen to hear him call you this, question him about it and hear his response. Or if you simply want to know what he'll say, catch him off guard with the question and ask, "Baby, am I your 'main thing'?" If he reassures you that you are his "only thing," then there you have it, but if he agrees that you are, you might want to speculate a little.

Sisters, if you are in a serious relationship with a man and he's introducing you as his friend to people he knows, then you might want to question him about that as well and get some understanding on just how serious of a relationship you are in because when a man introduces his woman, he'll do so claiming her, making it known that she belongs to him. See, if you and your man are out and he runs into a friend of his and introduces you, saying something like "What's up, John? How have you been, man? This is my friend Jane," then automatically his friend will know that you are just someone that his boy is with for the time being because of the word "friend." But say your man introduces you, saying, "What's up, John? How you been, man? This is my fiancée Jane, the love of my life," then his friend will know you are someone that his friend is taking seriously because of the affirmation his friend gave. You and your man may not even be engaged, but for him to come out and say those words let not only you know but his friend as well that he's serious about you. Men let other men know if they are serious about a woman by the words they speak of her. Men are good at doing this too, so good at it that you may never catch on or even notice it. So again, sisters, some advice I want you to remember is men are master manipulators. They know what to say, why to say it, when to say it and even how to say it. So don't let a man's words alone sweep you off your feet unless you know for sure that his words are sincere.

There's another type of name-calling I want to talk about in this chapter, sisters, which are those unhealthy names your man may be calling you. And each of you know exactly which names I'm talking about too (the Bs, Hs, Ws, etc.). If you and your man have a mutual understanding that the name-calling is out, great. But if the two of you don't have this understanding, and your man calls you everything but your name, I suggest you put a stop to it immediately and demand some respect because a man who truly cares for his woman will never disrespect her in any kind of way.

Sisters, if a man sees that you don't have enough respect for yourself to stop him from calling you out of your name, what in the world makes you think that your man will have enough respect for you not to cheat on you? It's simple—if you don't have respect for yourself, neither will your man. A man can and will only do to a woman what she allows him to do.

Once a man knows that he holds total control over the relationship, he will begin doing everything he pleases, knowing that he can get away with you finding out and not leaving him. And if you are willing to allow this, it means one thing, sisters: you are dependent on him. It doesn't always have to be his finances that you are depending on either. It could be his love or maybe the way he makes you feel a certain way. And this goes back to chapter 2,

"Loving and Believing in Yourself," because when you love and believe in yourself, you begin gaining knowledge about who you are and your self-worth. And knowing these things about yourself, sister, the BS you will not tolerate.

Sisters, if you are letting your man get away, *stop it*! And what I mean by get away is a lot of times, most of you will know that your man is out doing wrong but you call yourself loving him so much that you'll overlook his wrongdoings. STOP DOING THAT! Tell your man that you know what he's doing and either he straighten up his act or you're leaving. But you must mean what you say, sisters, and say what you mean. Point blank period. I know some things are easier said than done, but you have to think about it and consider what's more important to you—being truly happy or pretending to be happy just to be with somebody? By not settling, you honor yourself by staying true to your dreams and preserving the integrity of your purpose in life. There is no reason for you not to follow your heart.

Sisters, you have to be honest and authentic with *yourself* about the life you want to live.

Don't waste time trying to make things work with a man who doesn't want things to work himself, sisters. Move on with your life, and know that God will see that your soul mate finds you.

Another piece of advice I want to leave you with before I end this chapter is *never* dumb yourself down for a man, sister, meaning if you are headed somewhere in life and your man isn't (first of all, why are you with him?), he's not on your level, so don't stoop down to his level because doing so will eventually bring you down. I will admit that some men have small kinks in them that only a strong woman can straighten out to bring the best out of him. But don't be a fool trying to straighten these kinks out, sisters. A man who really has something inside of him will notice that his woman is destined for greatness and will become motivated to get up get out and get something to bring to the table as well.

Sisters, if you are the only provider for your family while protecting the family is your man's only asset, then now is the time to ask yourself, "Is He Worth It?"

"Men respect women who respect themselves and misuse and disrespect the ones who don't . . ."

It's sad but true, so respect yourselves, sisters!

About the Author

Keith L. Bell was born in Nashville on February 6, 1988 to Kerry L. Bell and Willie McLeod, along with two other siblings. He lost his mother

May of 2013 while incarcerated and working on "The Longest Drought Ever." He has been writing since 2007, penning his first novel. While he was incarcerated in 2011, his passion grew and turned into a desire to create stories that served as an escape from the stress of daily events.

Printed in the United States
By Bookmasters